My Allah Series

ALLAH IS EVERYWHERE

Kisa Kids Publications

AL-KISA FOUNDATION
WWW.KISAKIDS.ORG

Parents' Corner

فَأَيْنَمَا تُوَلُّوا فَثَمَّ وَجْهُ اللَّـهِ

Wherever you turn, there is the face of Allāh
(Sūrat al-Baqarah, Verse 115)

Dear Parents/Guardians,

One of the questions children frequently ask is "Where is Allāh?" This question is a sign of a healthy spiritual soul and indicates a desire to know Allāh and get closer to Him. InshāAllāh this book will help children understand that Allāh is always with them, as He Himself says, "...He is closer to him than his jugular vein" (50:16).

After learning that Allāh, who created us and loves us, is always with us, it is important to slowly start emphasizing that because Allāh is with us, we should *always* try to make good choices that He will be pleased with.

Allāh says in the Quran, "Does one not know that Allāh is always watching?" (96:14). If we can instill the notion, within ourselves and our children, that Allāh is always watching us, that He loves us and wants us to make the right choices to receive more of His blessings, inshāAllāh we can strengthen our *Taqwa* (God-consciousness).

With Du'as,
Kisa Kids Publications

When I was little, I thought Allah lived high up in the air.
So I climbed up a ladder to see if He was there. But then I started to understand that Allah is everywhere!

Where do you think Allah is?

Allah is on the mountains, in the valleys, and the lakes.
Allah is always with us, with every breath we take.

Do you need to climb a mountain to see Allah?

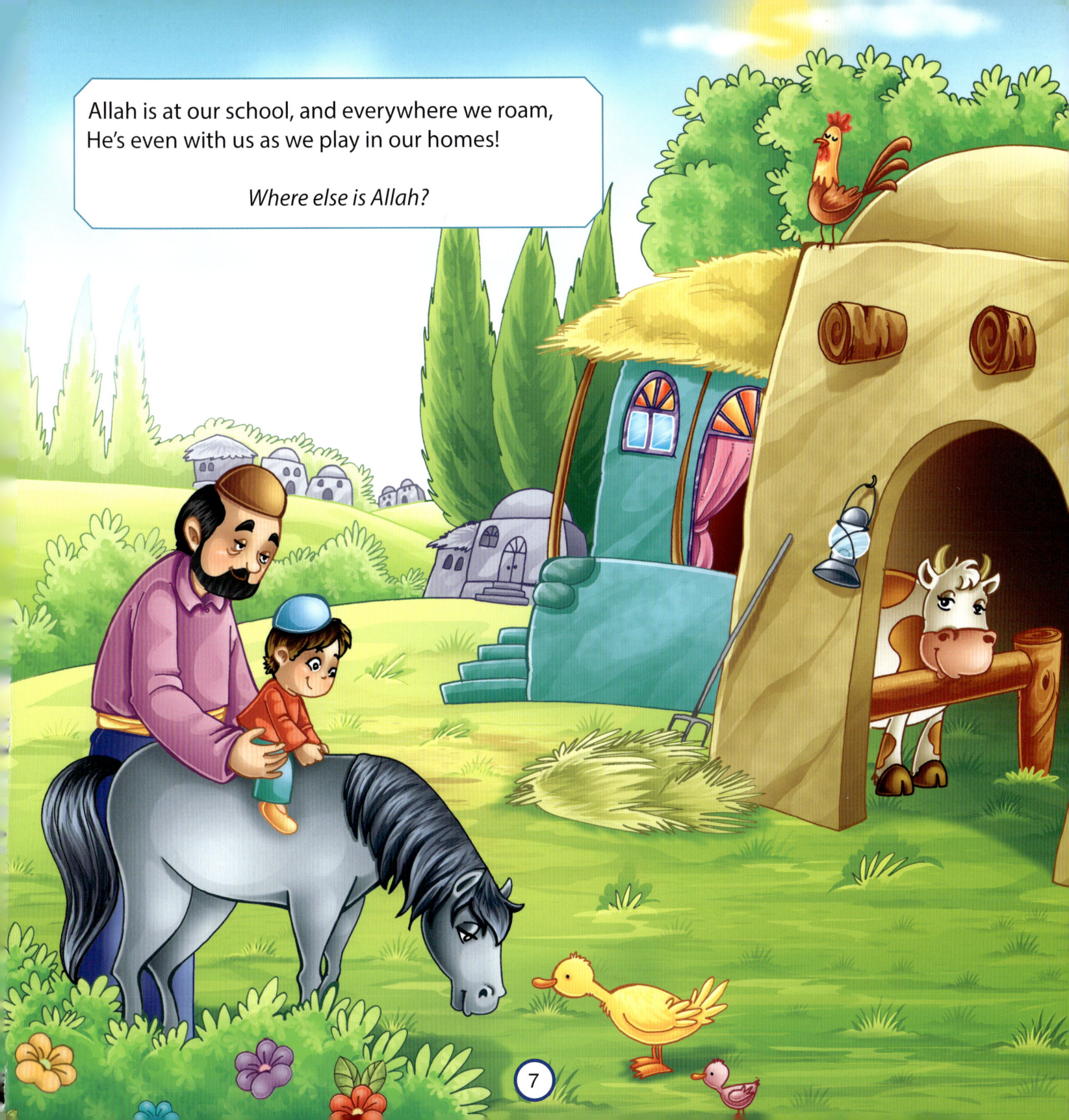

Allah made baby chicks so cute with perfect faces, hands, and feet. We know Allah is there when they pop out of their eggs and go "Cheep!"

Chicks are baby chickens. What other types of babies has Allah created?

Allah is always close to you, even as you read.
He'll always be your friend and give you everything you need.
So the more you love Him and do good deeds,
The closer you'll get to Allah with great speed.

What are some good deeds that can bring you closer to Allah?